WEALTH
MULTIPLIER

WEALTH
MULTIPLIER

The Proven Tax Efficient Strategy Used By The Wealthiest Canadian
Families to Create, Grow, and Protect Generational Wealth

ROBERT TRASOLINI
& LAURENT MUNIER

CERTIFIED

(H)

WRITTEN
BY HUMAN

DISCLAIMER

The information in this book is provided to educate and empower you as a successful entrepreneur seeking to make informed financial decisions. While we've done our best to provide insights and strategies that could be beneficial, it's important to remember that everyone's financial situation is unique, and this book is not a substitute for personalized professional advice.

We strongly encourage you to consult with trusted experts, such as financial advisors, accountants, or lawyers, to evaluate how the strategies discussed here apply to your individual circumstances. Tax laws, regulations, and financial strategies can vary based on location and change over time, so doing your due diligence is key.

Our goal is to provide you with the tools and knowledge to make the best decisions for your financial future. However, any actions you take based on this book are your responsibility, and we cannot be held liable for outcomes resulting from the use or interpretation of this information.

We're here to help you think differently about your financial opportunities and encourage you to use this information as a starting point for meaningful discussions with your financial team.

FOREWORD

Success in business is not just about making money, it is about keeping it, growing it, and using it wisely to enhance your own and your family's lifestyle. The challenge is not just building wealth; it is making sure it grows for you, your business, and your family for generations to come.

Like most successful entrepreneurs, time is my most precious and least available commodity. Being a veteran in finance, I have learned to quickly say 'No', and I am not shy to end a meeting quickly when I see the financial benefits are stacked against me. Over a decade ago, Robert and Laurent came to my office fully prepared to answer my tough questions and most importantly, their professional integrity was quickly transparent. At the end of that first meeting, I wrote a large cheque, and I was their first million-dollar account.

Since then, I have watched Robert and Laurent grow their business by advising the top entrepreneurs in Canada by helping these successful entrepreneurs turn financial success into lasting wealth. They know that growing a business is one thing, but strategically managing wealth is an entirely different game and is one that requires the right mindset, tools, and approach.

Many aspiring financial authors have pitched me on writing a foreword for their book. I have passed on all, until now. That is because I have personally used Robert and Laurent's services, and I have watched them struggle and succeed in growing their own business. Most importantly, they are individuals of high integrity. I think so highly of them, that I've even invited them over to my home to discuss business ideas with other successful financial experts and authors such as Robert Kiyosaki, who wrote the bestseller 'Rich Dad, Poor Dad' who would also agree with my endorsement of these two.

This book is not just about managing money, it is about creating personal freedom via financial independence, on your terms. Robert and Laurent are not here to sell a quick fix as there is no such thing in wealth creation. They are here to share a time-tested approach that will help you take control of your financial future and maximize the wealth you have worked so hard to build.

More specifically, the strategy explained in this book is used by the wealthiest families in Canada for over two centuries.

The Wealth Multiplier Account is not about speculation or taking unnecessary risks. It is a sophisticated but practical strategy designed to help business owners:

- Grow their wealth efficiently while maintaining full liquidity
- Seize new opportunities without unnecessary financial restrictions
- Create a financial legacy that stands the test of time

- Maintain control over their capital for both business and personal growth

This book is for the business owners who have already won round one building something great, and are now focused on playing the long game. Robert and Laurent do not just give you the map. They show you exactly how to use it.

Marin Katusa
Founder of Katusa Research, Fund Manager and
Best-Selling Author

CONTENTS

INTRODUCTION

Every entrepreneur suffers from the Fear of Missing Out…

You want to be at the forefront of your industry, capturing the right opportunities, leveraging the best strategies, optimizing everything you do to maximize your chances of success.

This drive to be the best you can be—and never miss out on the chance to do something better, faster, or smarter than you did yesterday—is what propelled you and your business to success.

So what if we told you that there's a huge missed opportunity sitting right under your nose?

And, what's more, that it isn't some newfangled, crackpot financial strategy that sounds too good to be true… It's one of the oldest and most trusted financial strategies in Canadian history. In fact, it's older than Canada itself. (Don't worry, we'll have a history lesson in Chapter 4).

We work with successful, ambitious entrepreneurs like you every day, so we can imagine the FOMO coursing through your brain from the moment we told you there's something you're missing out on. "What are these guys talking about? What's this strategy? Are my competitors using this? Why has no one told me about this?"

We don't want you to miss out, either.

That's why we wrote this book—to make as many Canadian entrepreneurs as possible aware of this strategy and how it can solve the problems of being too successful.

Yes, you read that right. Everyone talks about the challenges of building a business from scratch, but nobody talks about what happens after.

When your business becomes successful, you unlock a new level of problems.

What do you do with your retained earnings? How do you stop Ottawa from eating away at your wealth now that you're taxed at the highest rates? How do you accelerate your business's growth while maintaining liquidity?

And most importantly, how do you preserve and protect your wealth for your family, so that your business can leave a legacy to your loved ones for generations to come?

You don't need us to tell you that making money isn't just about making money. It's about what you do with that money—how you use it to enrich the lives of the people you love. You don't want your business's success, and the wealth it brought you, to begin and end with you. You want it to have a ripple effect through the generations of your family tree, giving your descendants the freedom and power to capture opportunities, build their own entrepreneurial endeavors, and leave a mark on the world.

Yet, when many successful entrepreneurs pass away, their families pay as much as 50% (or more) of what they inherit to Ottawa.

Do you want to be rolling in your grave, knowing those a**holes in Ottawa inherited 50% of the wealth you built over the course of your life?

You didn't work to build a business your whole life so that you could line some greedy politician's pockets… You worked so that, after you're gone, your spouse and kids would not only be taken care of, but inherit a financial legacy that will enable them to build something of value in the world.

The real tragedy when an entrepreneur's heirs lose 50% of the estate to taxes is that this is completely preventable if the entrepreneur had implemented the right strategy while they were alive.

In this book, we'll introduce you to that strategy.

You'll discover how countless entrepreneurs, for over 200 years, have been using this strategy to take back their financial freedom, accelerate their business growth, and preserve a financial legacy for generations to come.

Keep reading to find out what you've been missing out on…

CHAPTER 1

Champagne Problems™

Congratulations! You have a successful and profitable business. You have retained earnings being moved to your holding company each year. The kids are good. You bought that house. Everything seems to be going fine.

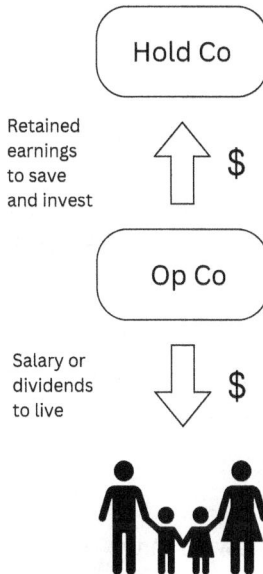

But you know what they say: "More Money, More Problems."

The problems you face today are different from the problems you faced yesterday.

Years ago, your problem was "How do I make my business successful?" Now, your problem is, "So my business is successful... What do I do now? How do I grow my retained earnings without them being subject to the highest tax bracket? How do I make sure I have liquidity for my business or for other investments that come up along the way? How do I pay for retirement without paying a massive amount in taxes? And at the end of it all, how do I transfer all of this to my family and loved ones to create a legacy?"

We like to call these problems Champagne Problems™—the problems that come as a result of success.

Grow It, Secure It, Use It, Pass It On

Now that you're successful, what will you do with your retained earnings? Grow it? Secure it? Use it? Pass it on?

Where are you keeping your money? In a bank account? In the stock market? Invested in real estate? You have to put your money somewhere... But choosing between the options now available to you can be overwhelming.

Your accountant and lawyer have done a great job to get you here – you are already incorporated, you already have or should have a holding company set up, and you have the right corporate structure for your protection and for tax efficiency – but what do you do with the profits? How can you grow these?

When you are incorporated and make up to $500,000 net income, you benefit from the small business tax rate, which is around 11% (but changes per province). After $500k in net, you are at the regular business income rate of 27% (depending on the province). This is why your accountant told you to incorporate in the first place.

If you were making this same amount of money personally, without incorporating, your marginal tax rate could be upwards of 50%.

Your accountant did an amazing job of saving you 30% - 40% in taxes by incorporating. But now what?

When you go to invest the money in your company, you have Champagne Problems™. When you go to take the money out, you have Champagne Problems™. When you want to leave the money to your kids, you have Champagne Problems™. And you are now a target of the government as a "greedy business owner who should pay more," as we will talk more about in Chapter 2.

Grow It

Will you grow your wealth by investing your business profits? What's the best way to invest–stocks, bonds, real estate, GIC, reinvesting in the business, or something else?

The challenge of investing within a holding company is that you're automatically taxed at the highest marginal tax rate. If you invest personally, you're taxed at a tiered rate based on your income.

To understand the impact of taxation on growing your wealth, let's imagine you double a dollar every day for thirty days.

How much would this dollar grow to at the end of 30 days—and how much would it grow to if you had to pay tax on it at a capital gains rate each time it doubled? (1/2 is taxable at 50% tax rate for easy number illustration)

Day	Without Tax	With Tax ($)	Difference (S)
0	1.00	1.00	0
1	2.00	1.50	0.50
2	4.00	2.25	1.75
3	8.00	3.38	4.63
4	16.00	5.06	10.94
5	32.00	7.59	24.41
6	64.00	11.39	52.61
7	128.00	17.09	110.91
8	256.00	25.63	230.37
9	512.00	38.44	473.56
10	1,024.00	57.67	966.33
11	2,048.00	86.50	1,961.50
12	4,096.00	129.75	3,966.25
13	8,192.00	194.62	7,997.38
14	16,384.00	291.93	16,092.07
15	32,768.00	437.89	32,330.11
16	65,536.00	656.84	64,879.16
17	131,072.00	985.26	130,086.74
18	262,144.00	1,477.89	260,666.11
19	524,288.00	2,216.84	522,071.16
20	1,048,576.00	3,325.26	1,045,250.74
21	2,097,152.00	4,987.89	2,092,164.12
22	4,194,304.00	7,481.83	4,186,822.17
23	8,388,608.00	11,222.74	8377,385.26
24	16,777,216.00	16,834.11	16,760,381.89
25	33,554,432.00	25,251.17	33,529,180.83
26	67,108,864.00	37,876.75	67,070,987.25
27	134,217,728.00	56,815.13	134,160,912.90
28	268,435,456.00	85,222.69	268,350,233.30
29	536,870,912.00	127,834.04	536,743,078.00
30	1,073,741,824.00	191,751.06	1,073,550,073.00

If Untaxed	If Taxed at Capital Gains Rate
$1,073,741,824.00	$191,751.06

As you can see, deferring capital gains tax could make a significant difference in your financial well-being.

The challenge with corporations is that there are not many ways to defer taxes on investment growth.

Secure It

Some business owners choose to leave their profit in a bank account instead of investing it. The thought process here is, "I work hard to generate a profit in my business, and I will generate more than what the stock market will generate. I don't want to let go of the money that's in my hands."

But leaving your money as cash rather than investing it is an enormous missed opportunity. With your money compounding in investments for years, it could generate millions of dollars… Why sacrifice that?

Also, if your money is sitting in a bank account, it's actually losing value every year due to inflation.

Many business owners are also concerned about securing wealth for their families. When you pass away, how do you ensure that your family is not only taken care of but can benefit from your business's financial legacy? How do you secure your wealth and success for generations to come? How can you maximize how much of your estate your family keeps and how much

Ottawa keeps? Later in the book, we'll cover how life insurance helps business owners secure their wealth and protect their family's finances.

Use It

A common theme we hear from business owners is: "I feel like the money in my holding company is trapped. I have $2 million in my holding company. If I pull $1 million out, I'm going to walk away with $500,000 because half of it is going to taxes."

As a business owner, you'll often want to use your money to buy necessary equipment/inventory for the business or to capture opportunities, such as purchasing other companies in your industry. To do this, you'll need to keep your money liquid. But when money is liquid, you're prevented from investing it or saving it for retirement. If you do invest your money, you can't access it when you need to use it for the business, which may prevent you from capturing rare opportunities or create cash flow issues. This conundrum leaves many business owners feeling stuck.

Pass It On

When you pass away, do you want the money your business generated to go to your kids and/or a charity of your choice? Or do you want the money to go to Ottawa, who will distribute it as they see fit?

Let's say you leave your holding company, with $10 million inside of it, to your kids. When they pull the $10 million out, they're going to pay more than 50% in taxes and lose $5 million to Ottawa. That's right, half of your estate is lost to the government.

How do you leave the money to your heirs in a tax-efficient way?

Your Surprise Business Partner... The Government

Whether you like it or not, one of your business partners is the federal government. Depending on how you set your business up, they could be a 20% partner, a 30% partner, a 40% partner, or even a 50% partner... How embedded do you want them to be in your business?

If you're not incorporated and you're making $1 million a year, you're a 50% business partner with the government.

We've seen this firsthand... Two guys in their early twenties had created an app that became the number one app in the App Store in their category. They had no business or job experience, were still living with their parents, and hadn't expected to have this level of success. They made $1.5 million dollars from the app, but they weren't incorporated... So half of that would be lost to taxes.

If they were incorporated, they would have paid 11% on their first $500,000 of net income and then 27% thereafter or a blended rate of 22% (depending on the province). They would have saved 28%-33% in taxes just by structuring correctly (any tax information is subject to change and differs from province to province).

These young entrepreneurs would have an extra $400-$500k in their pockets if someone would have given them good information to begin with.

There is a (completely legal) way to reduce the government's stake in your business, grow your wealth without losing it to taxes, have the liquidity you need to run your business and leave a tax-free legacy to your heirs upon your death... Later in the book, we'll show you how all of this can be possible.

So, these are the Champagne Problems™ you now face:

- You have retained earnings, and you don't know what to do with them. What's the best strategy to maximize your wealth?
- You want to invest your corporate money, but you're going to be taxed at the highest marginal rate (there are no RRSP or TFSA for companies).
- You want to pull the money out of your corp to spend or invest – but you're going to be taxed at the highest marginal rate. You would also need to sell your investments in order to access the funds, stopping funds from compounding.
- You need to keep liquidity for your business.
- How do you pass on wealth to your family without losing 50% to taxes?
- In all of these cases, you could end up paying ½ of your money in taxes if you don't do it right.
- We haven't even talked about the biggest Champagne Problem™ which will come in the next chapter – if you do invest your money and "make too much," now those

taxes are going to come after your operating company – welcome to the new Passive Income Rules.

All of these are expensive problems on their own… But combined with the new Passive Income Rules, they magnify even more!

CHAPTER 2

The Game Has Changed

You were told to play the game, but now the game has changed…

Game Changer #1: The Passive Income Rule

When the government implemented the Passive Income Rule, they painted successful business owners as villains. They sold the public on the idea that business owners are greedy, money-hoarding tax cheats who don't pay their fair share. You have advantages, they said, that the baristas and bartenders of the world will never have. And your greed? That's the cause of all society's problems.

Yeah, right. Any business owner can see through that spin. Doctors, lawyers, accountants, engineers, and entrepreneurs—the very people building the foundation of society—are suddenly cast as the bad guys. But this narrative worked. It allowed the government to justify introducing the Passive Income Rule under the banner of "fairness," while quietly rewriting the rules in ways that don't feel fair at all.

So, where did this Passive Income Rule come from? Enter Bill Morneau, Canada's finance minister at the time. Before stepping into politics, Morneau was the CEO of Morneau Shepell, one of Canada's largest providers of insurance and group benefits. He didn't just understand financial planning—he mastered it, running a company that specialized in products like life insurance and pension plans. Coincidentally, these are the same types of products that gained favor after the new rules came into play.

At the time, tax planning for business owners focused on strategies like income splitting and capital gains strips, which allowed for efficiency and reinvestment. The Passive Income Rule, however, made these methods less viable, instead steering business owners toward alternatives like life insurance—products Morneau Shepell conveniently offered. While we're not saying these changes were introduced for personal gain, it's hard to ignore how perfectly they aligned with Morneau's industry expertise. What we do know is that these rules forced business owners to rethink their strategies, shifting the financial landscape in ways that made growth and planning far more challenging.

Reduction in the Small Business Deduction Limit Based on Passive Investment Income

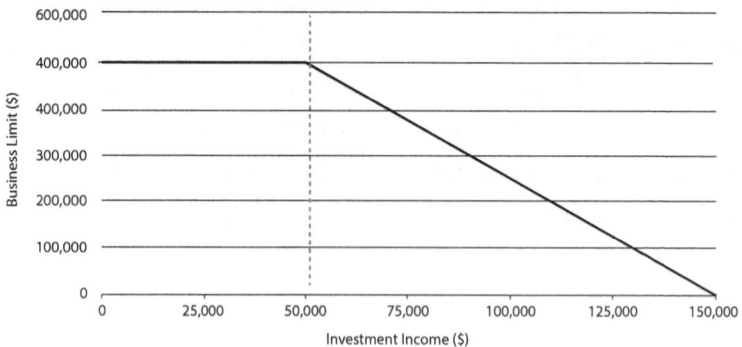

So what is passive income? With this rule, the government says that anything that is not directly your operating business is passive income. For example, if your business is a dry cleaner and you've invested in real estate or stocks unrelated to dry cleaning, that's passive income.

The government has said that if you make "too much" passive income in your corp or Holdco, it will take away your Small Business Deduction in a 1 x 5 ratio. For every $1 of passive income above $50,000, the government will take away $5 of your Small Business Deduction. Once you make $150,000 or more in passive income, you no longer have your lower tax rate Small Business Deduction on the first $500,000 in net.

Investing passively in your company automatically puts you at the highest capital gains rate, and when you invest corporately, you don't have tax-deferral opportunities like RRSP or TFSA.

Essentially, the Passive Income Rule changed the game so that if you want to grow your business assets through investing, you'll lose a significant portion of your Small Business Deduction which allows you to pay approximately 11% (depending on the province) in taxes.

What does this mean in real-life terms?

Take for instance the story of Warren, who is 42 years old, owns an engineering company, is married with two kids, and owns a home.

His operating company's net profit is $500k a year after paying himself $250k a year as a salary. His holding company has $3 million in retained earnings (adding $500k a year). The holding company's funds are invested for retirement in the next 15-20 years.

His operating company makes money, pays Warren his salary, and then the rest goes to the holding company for savings and investments. The operating company is taxed at the small business rate of 11% (in British Columbia). His personal marginal tax rate is 53%.

Let's say Warren has $3,000,000 in his holding company and he went to his local bank and bought a GIC at 5%. This would generate $150,000 of passive interest income for Warren's holding company. We are using an example of a GIC but this could have been income from real estate, bonds, or private debt that all would generate passive investment income as well.

What happens when we add taxes into the mix? The $150,000 earned from the GIC would be taxed as income so more than 50.67% of the $150,000 would go to tax. This would leave the company with less than $74,000 after taxes from this gain. The passive income received would grind down his small business deduction to 0 which would mean Warren's $500,000 of net income in his active business would be taxed at 27% instead of 11% costing him an additional 16% in tax or an additional $80,000 on the net income in his active business. When you add the two together this is more than $155,000 of tax owing as a result of this $150,000 of passive interest income. There are some benefits regarding what is called RDTOH and GRIP, which reduce the tax sting when pulling this money out of the corporation but for the purposes of this book we aren't going to go too deep into this. In this scenario there would be a refundable tax credit amount of $46,005 when distributing funds from the corporation however this only applies when funds are taken out of the corporation. Even considering the refundable tax credit the total tax bill on the $150,000 interest income would be over $110,000.

How can Warren:

- Grow his holding company savings in a safe and conservative way that he doesn't have to manage.
- Grow the money in his holding company tax-deferred.
- Keep liquidity so he can access funds now and later without nearly half going to taxes.
- Leave money to his loved ones or charity without nearly half going to taxes upon his death?

Later in the book, we will show you how Warren can do all of the above and more.

Game Changer #2: The Government Changed the Priority of Insurance vs Investments

Beyond the Passive Income Rule, the government has taken away many of the tools that were formerly used to deal with trapped and retained earnings.

Strategies such as Capital Gains Surplus Strip, Income Split, and Trust Planning used to be the go-to solutions that accountants and lawyers would turn to for their clients, but as the government took away these solutions, business owners were left to look elsewhere for solutions.

And Another Problem... Liquidity

You have the money and you want to make moves to grow it... But all of the recommended solutions to grow your money after the Passive Income Rule make you feel like your money would be trapped...

These recommended solutions include:

- Registered Retirement Savings Plans (RRSPs)
- Tax-Free Savings Accounts (TFSAs)
- Individual Pension Plans (IPPs)
- Holding your cash in the bank
- Investing in real estate

It's important to note most of the solutions are government-sponsored or registered programs.

Some of these recommended solutions have their benefits but won't solve every problem that a high-net-worth business owner faces. What if you need liquidity? What if your business has an emergency and you need $200k to stay operational? What if the stock market tanks 50%? What if you get an opportunity to buy your competitor?

In times like 2008 and 2020, it was difficult to get loans. If we experience another year like those, you'll want to have liquidity on hand so you aren't stuck trying to get a loan to operate or to take advantage of opportunities.

An individual pension plan can make sense in some cases, but most business owners don't want to tie their money up in a pension with onerous rules and restrictions. With your entrepreneurial vision, you want to have the liquidity available to chase opportunities and combat crises as needed. You don't want to be a prisoner to pension plan rules that may limit your ability to pursue opportunities and solve problems.

Afraid to lock their money up in the markets, many business owners keep it in cash in a bank account. This is an understandable response if you're afraid of losing liquidity, but keeping your value in cash is an enormous missed opportunity for growth.

Your money doesn't have to stay trapped in recommended solutions...

In Chapter 3, we'll introduce you to the Bullet Fund and Stacking Investments, two solutions that give you both liquidity and growth.

CHAPTER 3

The Paths Forward

What is Warren's path forward?

First, let's see what tax-advantaged withdrawal options Warren has–and the flaw with each potential solution:

Shareholder Loans	• These might not be available to Warren.
Capital Dividends	• He has to change his investment strategy to focus on growth and not capital gains—or switch to a buy-and-hold strategy to defer capital gains. *For example, if he owns rental properties as passive income, instead of paying off the building, maybe now he decides to maximize the mortgage and keep the building completely under debt so he can write it all off. Technically, all the income goes toward the mortgage, so he's "not earning."*
	• This approach may not provide the liquidity Warren needs.

Return-of-Capital Investments	• These may provide some tax advantages, but they also come with additional risks.

What the Government Wants Business Owners to Do?

Now, here's what the government wants business owners to do instead of investing through the business, which is now considered "passive income": Pay themselves an additional salary or dividends and invest personally through an RRSP or TFSA. These vehicles offer tax-deferred growth, and the RRSP reduces income tax payable now.

But the RRSP limit per year is $30,000, and Warren has $1 million ready to invest. That won't even move the needle.

Also, you don't want to have too much money in your RRSP because it creates a taxation problem down the line. Since the government is your partner here, they may not need the taxes right now, but that doesn't mean they won't take them eventually.

We're not anti-RRSP by any means—there's a time and place for it in a financial plan, and maybe Warren maximizes his $30k/year contribution. But it's a joke that the government proposed this as the end-all-be-all solution for business owners when most successful business owners have far more than $30k per year to invest.

When you put money into an RRSP, you get a deduction for that amount. Say you earned $100,000, and you put $20,000 into your

RRSP. Your taxable income would be $80,000. Later, when you take that money out in the future, you would pay taxes on the $20,000.

The theory behind the RRSP is that you're making more money now in your earning years, and you're in a higher tax bracket. Later, when you retire, you won't be making as much money, so you'll be in a lower tax bracket. That works for the majority of people. But no business owners we've talked to are trying to make less money later. They will probably be making more.

Another commonly recommended solution is a TFSA. You don't get a tax deduction when you put money into the TFSA, but it grows tax-free, and when you pull it out, it's tax-free. That sounds great... However, the contribution limit in 2024 is $95,000, with a maximum of $7,000 per year.

Everyone should likely have a TFSA, but if you're a business owner with income in the millions, $7k per year will not make a dent in the pile of money you want to save and invest each year.

What About IPPs?

You may also hear Individual Pension Plans (IPPs) mentioned by others as a possible solution. Let's take a look at the pros and cons...

IPP PROS

- Allows for higher employer tax-deductible contributions than RRSPs.

- Amounts within the IPP are generally protected from creditors.
- Allows for large lump-sum contributions through "past service funding" or "terminal funding."

IPP CONS

- Requires T4 income to qualify.
- Contributions are locked in and can only be withdrawn for retirement benefits.
- Subject to strict compliance requirements, including expensive actuary calculations.

The Individual Pension Plan is an old concept that was forgotten… Until the government introduced the new Passive Income Rule and proposed IPPs as a solution.

With an IPP, you're setting up a pension plan for your company. It allows you to contribute more than you could to an RRSP, but it's rigid and restrictive. You cannot take the money out except for when you're in retirement. An actuary has to calculate how much you can put in based on your age, income, and other factors (and you have to pay the actuary to do this).

The IPP is subject to pension legislation, and it requires a lot of work to comply with all the rules. And if you do it wrong, the penalties are huge. This might work well if you have, for example, a law firm with 20 partners. But if your business only has one or two owners, you won't want to tie yourself up in an IPP.

Beyond the Usual Solutions

Beyond these recommended solutions, your other options are:

- Just hold onto your money in a chequing account.
- Traditional investment portfolios: stocks, bonds, ETFs, mutual funds, etc.
- Real estate.

But as we've covered previously, tying your money up in a portfolio or real estate leaves you without the liquidity you'd need to take advantage of business opportunities. If you needed cash, you'd have to sell an investment. And leaving your money in the bank means it stagnates—and you miss out on the exponential growth it could have if invested.

After going through all of these options, it may seem like we've hit a dead end. You, as a high-net-worth business owner, must be doomed to one of these subpar solutions that keep your wealth from reaching its full potential, tie up your liquidity, or create needless headaches.

The Wealth Multiplier Account™

But there's one more solution we haven't unpacked yet... Meet the Wealth Multiplier Account™.

The Wealth Multiplier Account overpowers all of the solutions we've just covered.

Here's why:

- It's tax-exempt (growth doesn't count toward passive income rules).
- It uses a specially designed life insurance policy in which investments grow on a tax-deferred basis (no annual capital gains, dividend income, or interest income).
- Life insurance can be collateralized, providing immediate or future liquidity.
- Life insurance pays out tax-free and increases the Capital Dividend Account (CDA), which can pay to beneficiaries tax-free.

Here's how it works: Your holding company buys a specially structured, overfunded life insurance contract. It collateralizes this insurance contract to a bank. The bank lends the holding company the money as a line of credit that you can use to invest the money in your holding company while it remains in the policy. Your dollar is earning in two places at the same time.

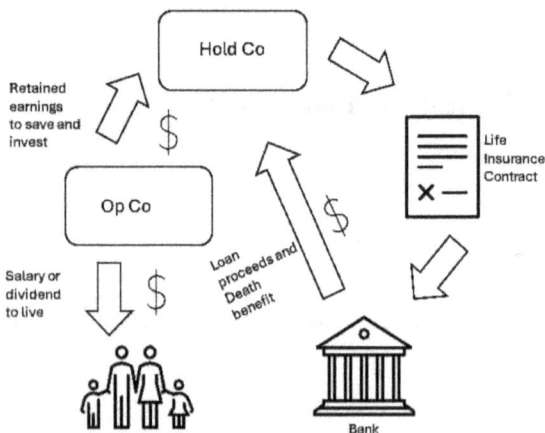

Hold Co

Retained earnings to save and invest

$

Op Co

Salary or dividend to live

$

Loan proceeds and Death benefit

$

Life Insurance Contract

X —

Bank

You have tax-deferred growth within the life insurance policy for the rest of your life, you get the interest deductibility on the loan when you use the proceeds to invest in income-producing investments, and now you get to make money twice on one dollar when you invest in another area.

Stacking Investments

If you want to grow your wealth, you take your money and buy assets. But if you want to amplify that growth, you can take those assets and buy even more assets.

This is the principle behind Stacking Investments. Essentially, you multiply your investments with the same dollar, growing your wealth exponentially.

It's like leveraging the equity in a property to buy another property, but instead of real estate, your collateral is a special type of insurance contract. It's simple and low maintenance—your insurance policy doesn't need new paint or a fixed roof!

The Bullet Fund

When opportunity knocks, a wise business owner has the cash ready to act. That's where your Bullet Fund comes in—a fund designed for quick access to capital so you can seize opportunities when they arise.

Picture this: During the 2008 credit crunch, those with Bullet Funds thrived while others couldn't access cash. They were buying assets at rock-bottom prices while everyone else was stuck.

Your Bullet Fund allows you to act without selling your current investments, putting you in a powerful position to capture game-changing opportunities.

CHAPTER 4

Why You Need Life Insurance

Every business owner, especially those of your caliber of success, needs life insurance.

Like it or not, we're all going to die someday. There's no way to cheat the system and get around this fact. So, knowing that death is inevitable, the best thing we can do for ourselves and our loved ones is to prepare for it via life insurance.

If you're married or have kids (or other family members, such as elderly parents, that you care for), life insurance provides for these people after your death. As a successful business owner making a large income, the loss of your income would be a tremendous financial blow to your family, so life insurance protects against this loss.

If you have a mortgage, those bills will still need to be paid after your death... Who will pay them? Life insurance eliminates the need for that question.

When you pass away, your money and assets, which represent the hard work and unique ingenuity that you contributed to the world, have to go somewhere. Without life insurance, much of this will get eaten up by taxes before it can pass to your heirs. But life insurance allows your estate to pass tax-free to your heirs, meaning that you can leave a legacy behind you.

The History of Life Insurance

Insurance companies are one of the four pillars of the financial system in Canada. Canada's financial system is built on banks, insurance companies, trust companies, and pension funds.

Banks accept deposits and make loans. They offer things like bank accounts, credit cards, loans, and mortgages.

Insurance companies provide protection in case things go wrong. The industry is split into two parts—general insurance and life insurance. General insurance covers stuff—like car insurance, condo insurance, business insurance, and boat insurance. Life insurance covers people—it provides protection against things that physically happen to you, like getting sick, injured, or passing away.

Trust companies specialize in trust, loan, and investment activities. They often hold the money that underlies investments and offer services like investment management, personal and business loans, and trust services for customers.

Pension funds are long-term investments offered by a company or government to provide retirement income for their employees. There are generally two types of pensions—defined benefit pensions and defined contribution pensions. There used to be more defined benefit pensions, but today, most of them are defined contributions.

Life insurance is older than Canada. There are actually some life insurance companies around today that have been around since before Canada became a country in 1867. At that time, insurance companies were included in the very creation of the Canadian financial system.

Due to this, life insurance has special tax advantages that you can't get anywhere else. The key one is that life insurance is tax-exempt, and the growth inside an insurance policy is tax-deferred. None of the other pillars of the Canadian financial system have these benefits.

This means that when life insurance pays out, that payout is tax-free. If your parents or grandparents have a life insurance policy, the benefit payout from that policy will be entirely tax-free.

The tax-deferred part means that when you put money inside a life insurance policy in Canada, that growth is tax-deferred. This means that you don't pay any taxes on that growth until you withdraw it. This includes whole-life policies and universal life policies. It also includes life insurance policies that you hold personally and life insurance policies that you hold inside a corporation or a trust.

The first life insurance company in Canada was the Canada Life Assurance Company, or Canada Life, which was founded in 1847. Canada Life is still around today and has over $500 billion in total assets under administration for over 17 million Canadians.

Another interesting bit of Canadian life insurance history has to do with Canada's first Prime Minister, Sir John A. Macdonald.

In 1887, after serving his term as Canada's first Prime Minister, he actually became the first president of a brand-new insurance company: The Manufacturer's Life Insurance Company, which we know today as Manulife. In the US, you'll know Manulife under their name, John Hancock Insurance.

Another interesting date in Canada's financial history is 1917, when Canada introduced the Income War Tax Act—which we now know as just the Income Tax Act. If you're super nerdy, the original income tax was 4% on anything above your personal exemption, which was $1,500.

This was supposed to be a temporary tax to pay for World War I, but it was made permanent in 1949 after World War II.

Life insurance is an important financial tool for Canadians, providing financial security and peace of mind for families in the event of the unexpected.

Life insurance companies in Canada paid out $14 billion in death benefits in 2020, over $36 billion in health benefits, and over $46 billion in retirement benefits. That's roughly $100 billion in total payouts to Canadians in one year.

Today, there are dozens of life insurance companies operating in Canada, and we work with most of the big ones.

From its beginnings in the 18th century to its current position as a key player in the financial system, life insurance has played an important role in protecting the financial well-being of Canadians for over 250 years. Not only is it older than your grandparents, but it is older than Canada itself.

Life Insurance Can Be Very Beneficial... If Done Well

Let's take a moment to recap all of the benefits of life insurance:

- You'll have life insurance coverage so that upon your death, there will be a payout to a beneficiary of your choice.
- It's tax-exempt.
- Banks will lend up to 100% of the cash value, so you'll have liquidity.
- Whole life insurance is not correlated with the stock market or real estate.
- Many Canadian insurance companies have a 100+ year track record of paying dividends every single year—that includes the World Wars, the Great Depression, stock market crashes, and COVID-19.
- Your money in a Canadian bank is insured up to $100,000. Your cash value in an insurance company is insured for $100k or 90% of the cash value, whichever is higher. For example, if you have $1 million in cash value and the insurance company goes bankrupt, you're insured up to $900,000. That's a big difference from banks... If you have $1 million in the bank and it goes bankrupt, you'd only get $100,000. And while banks are allowed to do fractional reserve banking and don't have to hold

all of your money on deposit, life insurance companies do. They're not allowed to lend more than they have in the way that banks do. Yes, banks are insured, but is the money really there? Meanwhile, insurance companies are required to have strong cash reserves. They must comply with the LICAT (Life Insurance Capital Adequacy Test) ratio. This means that life insurance companies are required to have enough cash reserves that if every single person with a policy died at the same time, they'd be able to pay it out.

Still trying to wrap your head around how much insurance companies have in reserves? If you go downtown in any major Canadian city, look inside the lobbies of major banks or commercial buildings… You're likely to see a plaque stating that the building is owned by a life insurance company. It doesn't make sense for banks to own the buildings they operate out of because they want to have the liquidity to lend more money. However, since life insurance companies are required to have so much in reserves, they can hold on to these valuable real estate assets and lease the space to banks or major corporations.

This is all great… But… If this is done poorly, it can be expensive or not effective for our purposes.

Life insurance has gotten a bad reputation because most advisors structure the policies poorly—in some instances because it benefits them.

How do you know if your whole life insurance policy is set up correctly for high cash values? If you have less than 50% of your premium deposit available as cash value in any of the first five years of your policy, it's a red flag that your advisor structured the policy incorrectly.

There are two types of participating whole life insurance: an estate version and a wealth version. Estate-type products are designed to maximize estate value—the ultimate amount of life insurance when you pass away—but they'll have little early cash value. Wealth products are designed to create the maximum amount of cash value early while giving you liquidity and remaining tax-deferred. You have to line up the right product with the right situation. You also have to take it a step further and make sure the policy is overfunded and with the correct insurance company.

If you want life insurance as an asset to use for tax-deferred growth while you're alive and you're sold an estate-focused policy, you'll be surprised to find that you have zero cash values for five or ten years, no investment component, and no liquidity, though you'll have a large life insurance payout upon your death. This doesn't mean that life insurance doesn't work—you were just sold the wrong type of policy.

If you were looking for liquidity and cash value, and you are simply buying the life insurance policy to leave the most amount of life insurance when you die with no need for liquidity or cash value, then an estate-type product might make sense.

The CRA knows that life insurance is tax-exempt, so they set a ratio of how much cash you can shelter in the policy versus how much life insurance you have, called the MTAR line (maximum taxable actuarial rate). The typical insurance advisor wants to sell you as much life insurance as possible, and they want you to pay as little for that policy as possible. But what ends up happening is that there's not a lot of tax-deferred cash value growth there. What you want to do is set up a low (but correct) amount of life insurance and as much cash value in the policy as possible.

However, a good advisor doesn't make recommendations for people without knowing their situation. The estate version of the plan may make sense for some people. There's a common trope on the Internet that the estate version of the plan is "evil" or a "scam" and that advisors who suggest it are only out for your money, but that's not necessarily true. It's only evil if the advisor knows that it doesn't make sense for the person's situation and convinces them to do it anyway.

So keep in mind, as we share information about wealth-driven life insurance products, that this is general information to help you understand how these products work, not a recommendation for one product over the other—you need to consult with a professional to determine which products are a fit for your unique situation and needs.

CHAPTER 5

The Wealth Multiplier Account™

The Wealth Multiplier Account™ is a specifically structured participating whole life insurance policy that is used inside a corporation to provide liquidity.

When life insurance pays out, it increases the capital dividend account (CDA) and allows those funds to go from the corporation to the individual all tax-free.

Most advisors are going to sell you as much life insurance as possible. Usually, they do this because they want to make the most amount of money selling you the biggest policy with no cash value. This is fine—as mentioned previously, you probably do need life insurance—but how can we solve more than one problem with the same product? Having ample life insurance and covering your estate needs on death is one concern, but what about all the other issues that we mentioned in previous chapters? That is why we have the Wealth Multiplier Account™.

We get you the right amount of life insurance that you need, and we want you to put as much cash as possible into the policy. We're putting in as much cash as possible without crossing the MTAR line. Traditional policies will have zero cash value for five years, but we want to see 80-90% cash values right away. Essentially, we're turning life insurance on its head.

Why do we do this? Well, life insurance has the big benefit of being tax-exempt. This allows the cash in the policy to grow on a tax-free basis. The growth in the policy also doesn't count toward the passive income rules.

Traditional advisors will tell you that you can use the cash value inside your policy if you ever have an emergency someday. But with the Wealth Multiplier concept, we get you access to use the cash values from day one.

Why Does the Wealth Multiplier Account™ Use a Whole Life Insurance Policy?

- **You need the life insurance anyway** and don't want to tie up your money in high premiums.
- **Life insurance in Canada is tax-exempt.**
- The **cash values inside your life insurance policy grow tax-deferred.**
- The **cash values inside your life insurance policy are safe, secure, and guaranteed.** This is why the banks will lend 80%, 90%, or even 100% loan-to-value against your cash values.
- At the end of the day, **life insurance pays out tax-free to your corporation or your named beneficiaries.**

So, you can grow your money inside the policy tax-free, you can access the money tax-free, and you can leave a legacy to your beneficiaries tax-free. No other financial instrument in Canada can do this. If we could use another type of asset or financial instrument to accomplish the same goals, we would.

Overall, the Wealth Multiplier Account™ allows you to grow your money tax-free, access your money tax-free, and leave your money to the next generation tax-free.

Why Use Whole Life Policies Rather Than Universal Life Policies?

There are a few reasons:

1. **Loan-to-Value Ratio:** Banks will lend a much higher loan-to-value ratio on the cash value in a whole life policy than they will on universal life policies. Universal life policies are invested in the market, so lenders will likely only lend 50-60% of the cash value. With a whole life policy, lenders are willing to lend 80%, 90%, or even 100% of the cash value.

2. **Stability:** Universal life policies are invested in the stock market, meaning you need to monitor them more regularly and adjust your investment mix as the market goes up and down. With a whole life policy, you set it and forget it. You can set it up today and not look at the investment component for the rest of your life.

3. **Risk:** A universal life policy has a lot of moving parts and more things can go wrong, while a whole life policy is solid and stable.

4. **Market Correlation:** Whole life policies are not correlated to the stock market, and your cash values are

immediately vested and guaranteed never to go down. With a universal life policy, your cash values are tied to the stock market and can go down.

Because the whole life policy is so safe, secure, and guaranteed, banks love to take these policies as collateral for lending. This is why we use participating whole life policies as the Wealth Multiplier inside your company.

Liquidity and Lending

The Wealth Multiplier Account™ is a safe, secure asset held by your corporation. Your money is growing safely, securely, and tax-free. However, now you want to use these funds for another investment, or your company requires capital to expand. Instead of selling your asset, stopping its compounding, and triggering taxation, we can instead take the asset to a third-party bank, and they will give you a loan for the full value.

One of the advantages of the Wealth Multiplier is the liquidity it provides. How we get this liquidity is by taking this corporate asset to a bank and setting up lending against it.

Now, you can't just walk into a bank branch and talk to a random teller to set this up. Loans against life insurance are done at the Private Banking level and the Commercial Lending level. Out of the tens of thousands of bank employees, only a very small percentage of them have any experience lending against life insurance policies. We work with the right people at all the major Canadian banks and can introduce our clients to the right private and commercial bankers to get this done.

Lending against your Wealth Multiplier life insurance policy is one benefit of using private banking. Some other benefits include:

- You have a direct relationship with someone at the bank who can handle all your personal and corporate business.
- You can call or email someone directly to get your banking done—no more 1-800 numbers or waiting on hold.
- They provide specialized lending for all your personal and company needs.
- You work with one professional and their team at the bank who know your entire financial situation—no need to re-explain your case every time.

Another benefit of working with a private banker is that they'll consider your corporate assets. Often, retail banks only look at your personal assets. This can be problematic if you have $10 million in your holding company but only pay yourself a moderate $100k salary. Though you're an ultra-high-net-worth individual, your personal assets don't reflect this, which can hinder your ability to get a mortgage or another type of loan. A private banker, meanwhile, will have an in-depth knowledge of your financial situation and would understand that you have valuable corporate assets.

When you borrow from a bank, the interest rates are more favorable, and there will generally be no taxation. Third-party banks will generally lend you up to 100% of the cash value of the policy, depending on your situation.

However, borrowing from a bank takes more work than borrowing from an insurance company. There is a credit check involved when you borrow from a bank, so the process isn't as seamless as borrowing from the insurance policy. There will also be full financial underwriting, annual reviews, and banking fees. With a bank, you don't get to set your own repayment terms—you have to comply with the terms the bank sets for you.

Though borrowing from a bank is more complicated, we can help you navigate it, so the burden is on us, not on you. Also, since different banks have different loan offers and credit requirements, we can help you determine which bank will be the best fit for you.

What Do You Do With the Money?

After we set up the life insurance policy and the loan, both of which have to be structured perfectly, there's a third step—what do you do with the money? How do we take advantage of the policy in the best way?

At this point, you can do whatever you want with the money: invest in your own business, invest in the market, invest in real estate, or even spend the money. Technically, you could blow the money on a Lamborghini and a trip to Vegas, but we don't recommend that.

If you want to be hands-off at this point, you can work with our wealth management service to handle the investing part for you so you don't have to spend time researching the best investments for your situation. We have a certified investment manager that we have partnered with and refer our clients to manage their money. However, if you are going to invest in the market, not all wealth managers are equal, so it's important to ensure you're working with a qualified professional.

CHAPTER 6

Three Benefits of the Wealth Multiplier Account™

You've set up your Wealth Multiplier Account™, your funds are growing with low risk in a tax-favorable way, you have life insurance coverage that protects your estate and family, and you have liquidity and access to all your capital. Now what?

There are three ways you can use your Wealth Multiplier Account™ to maximize its benefits:

Stacking Investments

With Stacking Investments, you earn in two places at once: inside the policy and on what you're buying.

Generally, most people can't earn money twice on one dollar. Banks achieve this through fractional reserve lending, and people who own assets they can borrow against, such as real estate, can do this. For the average person, however, leveraging a life insurance strategy like this is the only way to stack investments and earn in two places simultaneously.

Many people associate Stacking Investments with real estate. For example, real estate investors often buy a property, wait for it to appreciate in value, and then leverage it to buy another property.

This is one example of Stacking Investments, but the key difference in doing this within a life insurance policy is that your money grows in two places: inside the policy and in your investments.

- **Example 1:** One client runs a private lending firm. He funds his life insurance policy, borrows against it at favorable rates, and reinvests the borrowed funds into his lending portfolio, earning higher returns than the interest on the loan. Additionally, because the loan is used for investing, the interest may be tax-deductible, offsetting some passive income gains. Meanwhile, the original funds inside the policy continue growing tax-deferred.
- **Example 2:** Another client owns mobile home parks, which are challenging to secure traditional financing for. She borrows from her policy to access capital quickly and purchase more parks. By leveraging the policy, she gains an edge in a competitive market, allowing her to scale her portfolio faster than competitors who rely solely on banks.
- **Example 3:** A third client runs a high-capital business requiring significant inventory purchases. By using Stacking Investments, he deposits funds into his insurance policy, where they grow securely, and then borrows against the policy to finance his operating expenses. This strategy provided the liquidity he needed while still saving for the future.

With Stacking Investments, you get the best of both worlds: dividends and leverage.

The Bullet Fund

One client came to us a few years before the market crash in March 2020 and said, "The market is too hot. I know it's bound to crash eventually, and when it does, I want to be ready to buy while my competitors aren't."

He wanted to diversify his equity-heavy portfolio and prepare for future opportunities. After selling his business, he deposited part of his proceeds into his life insurance policy, which began growing tax-deferred.

When COVID-19 hit and the stock market crashed, he used his policy as a Bullet Fund, borrowing $1 million to buy dividend-paying stocks while the market was at its lowest. The dividends from his investments exceeded the loan interest, and as the market rebounded, he sold some stocks at a profit to repay the loan while keeping the portfolio intact.

Without the Bullet Fund, he wouldn't have had the liquidity to seize this once-in-a-lifetime opportunity.

The Bullet Fund ensures you're ready to act when opportunities arise, giving you liquidity without forcing you to sell assets or rely on bank approval.

- **Buying a Competitor:** If your competitor is in distress, a Bullet Fund allows you to act quickly and purchase their business, scaling yours without waiting for bank approval.
- **Purchasing Equipment:** Banks may hesitate to lend full value for equipment purchases, but a Bullet Fund allows you to pay in cash and grow your business without delays.
- **Real-Time Opportunities:** Whether it's discounted real estate, undervalued equipment, or a struggling competitor, the Bullet Fund puts you in a position to outmaneuver others.

With the Bullet Fund, you can make decisive moves while others are still waiting for bank approvals.

The Secure Retirement Plan™

So far, we've focused on using the Wealth Multiplier Account™ during the accumulation phase of life. But this strategy also enables you to supplement your retirement income in a tax-advantaged way.

When you set up your policy, you're likely in your 30s, 40s, or 50s and have years of investing ahead. You'll borrow from the policy to invest in real estate, markets, or your business. But eventually, when you retire, you can use the policy to create a Secure Retirement Plan™.

Once you reach retirement age (usually 50–60 depending on the bank), you can convert your loan into a retirement income stream. Instead of making interest payments, the bank will defer repayment until your death, deducting the loan from your policy's death benefit.

Here's how it works:

- **Example:** Warren has $10 million in his policy at retirement and borrows $500k annually for 20 years, accruing $15 million in total debt. When Warren passes away, his policy has grown to $24 million, and the death benefit covers the $15 million owed to the bank. His beneficiaries still receive $9 million tax-free.

With this strategy, Warren enjoys tax-free retirement income while preserving wealth for his heirs. No other financial instrument offers this level of flexibility and tax efficiency.

> **Disclaimer:** These are examples for educational purposes. Consult a professional to tailor this strategy to your unique situation.

CHAPTER 7

Your Team Matters

Who is on your team? If you want your financial plan to succeed, you need to have quality people on your team. Your team members should be open to communicating and collaborating with the other members of your team—a professional who works in a silo and fails to "zoom out" to the bigger picture will only get in the way of your goals. If you want to maximize the benefit of the Wealth Multiplier Account™ or any aspect of your financial life, you need a good team.

Not all professionals are equal. In this chapter, we'll break down the types of professionals you need on your team and what qualities to look for in each.

Accountant

In the entire scope of their education, accountants get only a couple of hours of training on life insurance. Most accountants will not have heard of this strategy, let alone have training in how to execute it properly. Because of this, you want an accountant who is open to new ideas and collaborating with other professionals.

Most accountants are focused on the past—they look at your taxes from the previous year and help you file them. While this is useful, a truly valuable accountant will look towards the future. Not only will they help you reconcile last year's taxes, but they'll make recommendations with an eye to minimizing your future taxes. A forward-looking accountant will ask you questions about your future: What are your goals? Are you buying a house? Are you selling your business? Are you getting married? Are you having kids?

You want to look for a business tax accountant. Just as attorneys have different niches, so do accountants, so don't assume that every accountant has the same range of knowledge.

Lawyer

You want to work with a business and/or tax lawyer—not a lawyer who handles divorces or personal injury cases. It's a plus if this lawyer specializes in high-net-worth individuals or business owners in your industry.

Have you outgrown your lawyer? The business lawyer you worked with on day one may have been great for where you were when you started your business, but as your business has grown, you may have outgrown your lawyer's capabilities and specialization.

Investment Advisor

What is a good investment advisor? A good investment advisor is someone you have a strong relationship with and trust. They take the time to understand you and your situation rather than just crunching numbers and providing generic solutions. They offer proactive advice about the future rather than waiting for you to call them. They understand the big picture of your financial life and are willing to work with the rest of your team.

Is your investment advisor willing to work with other professionals, or do they see other professionals as competition? Some investment advisors have the mindset that you're only allowed to invest in what they recommend, viewing outside investments as a threat. If an investment advisor discourages you from making investments that are in your best interest, it's a red flag that they're more focused on their profits than yours.

Often, bank investment advisors are not allowed to refer clients to any outside investments and are pressured to collect as many assets as possible. This makes working with a bank investment advisor usually a poor choice. Additionally, banks have high employee turnover, meaning you may have a different advisor every few months. Within this system, it's nearly impossible to build a lasting relationship with an advisor who truly understands your needs. Advisors who stay with banks long-term are often those unable to move beyond that environment.

Were you assigned your advisor, or did you have the opportunity to choose someone you like and trust?

Banker

Do you have a banker, or do you simply walk into the bank and talk to whoever is available?

95% of bankers won't understand the Wealth Multiplier Account™ strategy. Ideally, as a high-net-worth individual, you should work with a private banker. With a private banker, you won't waste time re-explaining your situation to a new representative or waiting on hold for 45 minutes to get a question answered. A private banker familiar with your situation and readily available is essential for any successful business owner.

Insurance Professional

Every business owner needs a traditional insurance professional to handle property and casualty (P&C) insurance and general liability for their home, automobile, business, and other personal liabilities. This professional ensures you're protected from a risk perspective. You may have multiple professionals in this role with various specializations. If your business operates in a high-risk industry, such as construction, medical, or transportation, you'll want to work with a P&C insurance professional experienced in your specific industry.

Beyond this, you need a separate life insurance professional specializing in corporately held life insurance. Traditional insurance professionals are generalists, but to effectively use the strategies outlined in this book, you need someone specifically trained in this niche.

Traditional insurance professionals insure stuff—boats, cars, houses—while life insurance professionals insure people.

There's a reason why the life insurance industry has a stigma. Some companies operate as multi-level marketing (MLM) schemes in the insurance space. Avoid these companies and advisors who treat life insurance as a side hustle. Your situation is too complex for their limited expertise. To find a qualified professional, look for someone who works in life insurance full-time.

Core Values to Look For

When selecting professionals for your team, ask yourself:

- How involved is this professional in their industry?
- Do they practice what they preach?
- Are they staying up to date on trends in the industry and the market?

A quality professional should have these traits:

Relationship-Focused

A relationship-focused professional won't rush to make a transaction. Instead, they'll take the time to understand your needs and ensure the solutions they implement align with your goals. They assume you'll be a client for at least ten years, if not a lifetime, and act accordingly. If someone is too eager to close a deal without fully understanding your situation, they're likely prioritizing their profits over your success.

Independent

An independent professional has no obligations to a specific bank, insurance firm, or investment company. They're free to recommend what's best for you without being influenced by quotas or corporate goals.

No Pressure, No Rush

The financial industry often has a reputation for being pushy, but a quality professional will never pressure you into a decision. Instead, they'll educate you, provide you with the information you need, and leave the ultimate decision in your hands. If someone pressures you to sign before you're ready, it's a red flag.

If you have a gap on your team, don't worry... We can help. One of the ways we add value for clients is by introducing them to high-quality professionals who are committed to client success, experienced in working with high-net-worth individuals, and open to applying the Wealth Multiplier Account™ strategy.

If you need help building your team, feel free to reach out to us at Robert@safepacific.com
www.safepacific.com

CHAPTER 8

Your Customized Voyage™

If you want your wealth multiplication strategy to be effective, you can't just jump into buying a product. You need to work with an advisor to understand where you are and where you want to go so that you can select the products and strategies that are right for you. At SafePacific, we call this the Wealth Multiplier Discovery Meeting™. This process helps determine if this concept even makes sense for you. If it doesn't, we'll let you know.

The Problem with Traditional Advisors

What does this process look like with a traditional advisor? A traditional advisor will likely ask for your basic information:

- How much do you make?
- Are you married?
- What is your house worth?
- Do you have a mortgage?

After collecting these facts, the advisor will try to create a plan. But wait a minute... This advisor knows nothing about how you view money, what your goals are, or what matters most to you. How can an advisor create an effective plan without understanding who you are, how you think, and what you want?

Money is emotional, and it means different things to different people. Unless we know what it means to you, how can we make a meaningful recommendation? For example, some people can't sleep at night if they owe even a single dollar on their mortgage. Even if the numbers show that leveraging productive debt would benefit this person, the strategy would only cause anxiety, leading to potential mistakes that disrupt their plan.

The Wealth Multiplier Discovery Meeting™

Our Discovery Meeting™ has four parts:

1. **Where are you today?**
   o We collect your vital statistics.
2. **What are your goals and concerns?**
   o Where do you want to go?
   o What do you want to avoid on your way there?
3. **How do you think about money?**
   o What is your philosophy?
4. **Who is on your current financial team?**
   o Who else are you taking advice from?
   o Are you happy with your current team, or would you like us to connect you with new people to fill roles on your team?
   o How do you see us fitting in?
   o How do you prefer to receive information (calls, texts, email)?
   o What do you expect from us? What defines success?

We'll also unpack how you learn so we can figure out how to best communicate information to you. Some clients need visuals to understand financial concepts, others prefer written documents, and some just want high-level summaries. Engineers, for example, often prefer to analyze every detail before moving forward.

We ask 50+ questions during this meeting. It typically takes about an hour, but we'll take as much time as needed to fully unpack your answers and understand how we can serve you.

Why spend the time to answer these questions? Why not just take ten minutes to show you a product and make a sale? The plan we're setting up for you is a **lifetime plan**. The strategies we implement will be in place for decades, and we'll ideally work with you for the rest of your life.

You need to like and trust us, and we need to like and trust you. It's worth investing the time upfront to get to the root of who you are and what you want before creating a plan that affects your finances for the rest of your life. We don't want to rush into a plan and hear ten years later that it's not working because we cut corners.

Sometimes, Your Customized Voyage™ doesn't include us. We may find that you're not a fit for us. If that happens, we'll still add value by giving you recommendations for improving your financial situation and connecting you to other advisors who might be a better fit.

Charting Your Voyage

Most people leave meetings with traditional advisors feeling more confused than when they walked in. At Safe Pacific Financial Inc., our goal is to make the complex simple.

Rather than giving you a 40-page document full of jargon, we'll provide a one or two-page customized proposal that summarizes:

- What's important to you.
- What your goals are.
- Our high-level recommendations.

We'll explain each option in layman's terms—how it works and why it's a good fit for your needs. If you want the detailed 40-page document, we're happy to provide it, but most business owners prefer the simple version. You've hired us to handle the complexities so you can focus on running your business.

The Next Steps

After going through the Wealth Multiplier Discovery Meeting™ process, clients often feel a deep sense of trust and understanding. Most people rarely talk about their hopes, dreams, fears, and philosophies—especially with a financial advisor—so this process can feel like a breakthrough. And by this point, after two meetings, you haven't owed us a dime.

Past the discovery phase, once we've agreed on a solution, the process is simple. We handle the legwork—completing paperwork, underwriting, setting up life insurance, opening investment accounts, connecting with banks, and reaching out to accountants—so you can stay focused on your business.

Take a moment to reflect on your experiences with your current or past advisors:

- How did you feel after your last meeting? Did you understand their recommendations?
- Did your last plan feel customized or cookie-cutter?
- Do you feel like your advisor truly knows you, or were you just "sold" something?
- Do you have buyer's remorse?

A financial plan should give you confidence and security, knowing it's leading you toward the future you want. If your current advisor hasn't given you that sense of confidence, it's time to move on.

CHAPTER 9

Take Control of Your Money

Remember our business owner, Warren? Let's take a look at what his life is like after implementing the Wealth Multiplier Account™:

- Warren invests $10 million ($500k annually for 20 years) in a tax-sheltered life insurance policy.
- Growth inside the policy is exempt from passive income rules.
- Funds grow on a tax-deferred basis, so Warren doesn't pay tax on dividends received.
- Warren can access funds now or later via a loan, which doesn't trigger capital gains.
- Warren uses the funds to supplement his retirement income.
- When Warren dies, the life insurance pays out tax-free to his corporation, increasing the Capital Dividend Account and allowing the funds to flow to his beneficiaries tax-free.

Note: The CDA is calculated by the ACB minus the NCPI. Depending on timing, the death benefit may exceed the CDA created.

Warren has taken control of his money, allowing him to accomplish more of his goals while securing his financial future. That's an enormous win.

Building a Strong Foundation: Dr. Bob's Story

In our practice, we've had the privilege of working with many clients, but Dr. Bob stands out as a remarkable example of how strategic planning can transform finances. Bob, a dedicated family physician, built a thriving medical practice after years of hard work. Yet, like many high-income earners, he faced challenges with taxes, retirement planning, and securing his family's financial future.

When we met Bob, he felt overwhelmed by the complexities of managing his wealth. He wanted to maximize savings and leave a meaningful legacy for his children but struggled with the tax burdens and investment risks that hindered his progress.

Growing up, Bob faced financial hardships, including the loss of his father, who hadn't left financial support or life insurance. Determined to create a better future for his own family, Bob sought a strategy to:

- Grow his wealth,
- Access his wealth,
- Leave his wealth—all tax-free.

How the Wealth Multiplier Account™ Helped Bob:

1. **Tax-Free Growth:** By funding his policy, Bob's investments grew tax-deferred, enabling him to accumulate wealth more effectively and prepare for retirement.
2. **Access to Cash:** Bob could take loans against his account without triggering taxes, providing flexibility for emergencies or investment opportunities.
3. **Family Protection:** The policy's death benefit ensured Bob's family's financial security in case of his untimely passing, giving him peace of mind.
4. **Legacy Planning:** The tax-free death benefit structured a significant inheritance for his children, empowering them to pursue education, purchase homes, or start ventures.
5. **Passive Income Opportunities:** Bob leveraged the policy's cash value to invest in assets like real estate or dividend stocks without incurring tax penalties. He also used the cash value to help fund his retirement goals without needing to sell other assets.
6. **Navigating Tax Rules:** The Wealth Multiplier Account™ helped Bob mitigate passive income tax rules and capital gains tax impacts, preserving and growing his wealth.

Over the years, Bob diligently funded his policy, watched his cash value grow, and used it strategically for investments. Whenever a new opportunity arose—whether it was a real estate investment or an upgrade for his practice—Bob accessed his cash value instead of liquidating other investments or taking on excessive debt.

With the Wealth Multiplier Account™, Bob was able to maximize his retirement savings while ensuring that his children and grandchildren would not face the same struggles he did. The tax-deferred growth and access to cash allowed him to build substantial wealth, providing peace of mind knowing he could support his family.

As Bob approached retirement, he felt confident stepping back from his practice, knowing he had laid a solid financial foundation. He envisioned a future filled with travel, volunteering, and quality time with family—all while ensuring that his children would inherit a legacy that could empower them in their own lives.

Bob's story is a testament to the power of informed financial planning. By embracing the Wealth Multiplier Account™, he transformed not only his financial outlook but also the security and opportunities available to his family. Through his journey, we see that with the right knowledge and tools, anyone can navigate the complexities of finance and create a brighter future.

A Life Without Regrets

Business owners who implement the Wealth Multiplier Account™ enjoy unparalleled financial security. Their wealth grows without market volatility, and they can access funds when needed without triggering major tax events or asset sales.

- **Reduced Tax Burden:** With lower taxes, business owners keep more of their earnings, reinvest in growth, and accelerate success.
- **Flexibility in Opportunity:** The Bullet Fund ensures you're ready to invest when others can't. Beat competitors

to prime opportunities and make deals that amplify your growth.

- **Freedom to Act:** Access to capital when you need it— whether mitigating a crisis or seizing opportunities—is invaluable in ensuring long-term success.

For successful business owners, wealth isn't just about numbers— it's about impact. Your ingenuity and ambition deserve to be rewarded with strategies that empower growth rather than complicate life. The Wealth Multiplier Account™ helps you:

- Achieve your goals without regrets.
- Secure your personal and family's financial future.
- Build a legacy that benefits loved ones or causes you care about.

You worked hard to build your business; don't let taxes or missed opportunities hinder your success. With the Wealth Multiplier Account™, your wealth grows tax-free, your retirement is secure, and your legacy is protected.

It's time to take control of your money.

If you're ready to explore how the Wealth Multiplier Account™ can help you achieve your goals, reach out to us today at
robert@safepacific.com
laurent@safepacific.com
safepacific.com/discovery-schedule

Let's build your zero-regret financial strategy together.

ABOUT THE AUTHORS

Robert Trasolini, PFA Advisor Vancouver | Safe Pacific

Robert was born and raised in Vancouver and began his career as an advisor in 2010. He has since founded Safe Pacific Financial Inc with the mandate to build long term trust by giving the best advice and service possible to his clients. The company was built on the philosophies of independence, relationship focus, with no pressure, and no rush.

Robert has specialized in working with business owners and professionals in the Vancouver area. He is most passionate about working with his clients to better understand their financial situations. Robert believes that by uncovering their goals, and the potential challenges they may face, he is able to proficiently help clients achieve their objectives.

When Robert is not working he spends time with his wife and two year old daughter. He also enjoys biking the sea wall, playing beach volleyball and enjoying the outdoors. Robert is licensed to serve clients in BC, Alberta and Ontario.

Laurent Munier, PFA Advisor Vancouver | Safe Pacific

In 2011, Laurent founded his fifth company, Safe Pacific Financial, to help Canadians achieve their financial dreams. He's been living the Canadian dream since immigrating here at 5 years old. His work life started with a paper route in the 3rd grade and he's been working and building ever since.

The "Why" behind launching Safe Pacific is to work with great people, add value to both their business & personal life and demystify the convoluted world of finances so they can focus on being the best at what they do for their families, companies and community.

Laurent's personal work philosophy is simple: Independent, relationship focused, no pressure, no rush. He loves working with like-minded and motivated people that strive for success every day.

Laurent gives back to the industry by volunteering his time and expertise on the Vancouver board of Advocis – The Financial Advisors Association of Canada where he won Volunteer of the Year award for 2019. Laurent is licensed to serve clients in – BC, Alberta and Ontario.

www.ingramcontent.com/pod-product-compliance
Lightning Source LLC
Chambersburg PA
CBHW070944210326
41520CB00021B/7051